# Cheslin Kolbe

## ROAD TO GLORY

### Jeremy Daniel

Jonathan Ball Publishers

JOHANNESBURG · CAPE TOWN · LONDON

Originally published in South Africa in 2021 by
JONATHAN BALL PUBLISHERS
A division of Media24 (Pty) Ltd
PO Box 33977
Jeppestown
2043

ISBN 978-1-86842-949-3
eBook ISBN 978-1-86842-950-9

*Every effort has been made to trace the copyright holders and to obtain their permission for the use of copyright material. The publishers apologise for any errors or omissions and would be grateful to be notified of any corrections that should be incorporated in future editions of this book.*

Website: www.jonathanball.co.za
Twitter: www.twitter.com/JonathanBallPub
Facebook: www.facebook.com/JonathanBallPublishers

Cover by Johan Koortzen
Design, typesetting and illustrations by Johan Koortzen

Set in 13 on 18pt Bembo MT Pro

# Contents

# CHAPTER 1

# *CHESLIN – A SPRINGBOK CHAMPION*

The roar of the crowd was deafening. The lights seemed to shine brighter than ever, and it felt as though every camera and microphone on earth was pointing directly at the field. Cheslin Kolbe, can you believe it? Here you are – standing on the field in Japan's Yokohama Stadium, seconds away from playing against England in the 2019 Rugby World Cup Final! Cheslin almost pinched himself to check whether it was real.

For as long as Cheslin could remember, this had been his dream. Morning after morning, training towards this goal had pulled him out of bed and into the gym. Now, as he looked around at the packed stadium, the wall of cameras and the cheering fans, he realised just how much he had achieved.

The Springboks were considered the underdogs against England in this match. Only a week earlier, England had been unstoppable against New Zealand's All Blacks in the semifinals, whereas the Springboks had had to work hard to beat Wales.

But Cheslin knew that anything could happen in a final.

He and his teammates lined up to sing the National Anthem and give each other some last-minute motivation, and then the game was on. At these big games, the pre-game tension was so enormous that it was a relief when the whistle blew and the flyhalf hoisted the ball into the air.

From the start, the South Africans played beautifully. In scrum after scrum, the dominant forward pack shoved England backwards, forcing them to make errors and give away penalties. At half-time the Boks were leading 12 points to six, thanks to four pinpoint penalty kicks from Handré Pollard and some fierce defending – especially from Faf de Klerk and Cheslin, both of whom were bringing down players double their size.

As the pressure on them mounted, England kept making mistakes and the Springboks kept growing more confident.

Back home in South Africa, thousands of rugby fans sat glued to screens and radios, as the excited voice of the commentator blared out: 'It's the 66th minute, and the ball is out on the left wing. Makazole Mapimpi chips it beautifully over the defence. It's gathered by Lukhanyo Am, who takes a few paces and delivers a no-look pass back to Mapimpi … and Mapimpi goes over for the first try of the match! The crowd is going wild, and the Boks are looking unstoppable!'

By the 74th minute, the Springboks were ahead by 25 points to 12. With only six minutes to go, it looked like a sure win for South Africa.

After a crunching tackle on the halfway line, one of the English players dropped the ball. It was scooped up by Lukhanyo Am, who offloaded it into the arms of Pieter-Steph du Toit, who passed it out quickly to Cheslin. The pass was a little too high but Cheslin adjusted instantly, jumping to gather the ball without breaking his stride. He had some space ahead of him, so he sped up, all the time keeping a close watch on two large English players who were stalking him.

Cheslin feinted to the left, sold a dummy, stepped right, then left, and burst through the arms of England's captain, Owen Farrell. It was the kind of move he was famous for and it left England's defenders looking like amateurs. In seconds he was ahead, over the line and dotting the ball down firmly.

Cheslin pumped his fist in victory as he jogged towards the crowd. At that moment, all the fight went out of the English team.

A few minutes later, the final whistle blew, the crowd roared their approval and the dream became reality. South Africa had won the 2019 Rugby World Cup with a score of 32 points to 12. The shocked and grateful players hugged each other, many in tears. Some fell to their knees. For every member of the squad, this was the biggest moment of his career.

Cheslin spent the next few hours in a daze. The medals were handed out and South African captain Siya Kolisi triumphantly held up the gleaming trophy. There was singing and dancing, phone calls from family and friends, handshaking, high-fiving, backslapping and congratulations from celebrities and dignitaries. Cheslin felt dizzy with emotion and the non-stop joyful whirlwind of celebrations.

As he lay in bed much later that night, Cheslin thought about the expressions on the faces of his teammates and coach in that final moment of the game. They had put so much faith in him, and he was deeply grateful to have rewarded them with a great performance. Everyone had played their part perfectly.

Cheslin knew that everything changes after you become a world champion, but it was only when the Springboks arrived back in South

For everyone in the squad, this was the biggest moment of his career.

Africa that he experienced what that meant.

At the airport, a huge crowd of excited fans was waiting – black and white, men and women, old and young – and they were all dancing and singing together. Most people in the country had had a tough year and needed some good news. The Boks had given it to them and now they wanted to celebrate.

Two days later, the team started on a tour around the country. They drove by bus from Pretoria to Johannesburg and Soweto, where cheering crowds followed them every step of the way. The players smiled and waved from the open-topped bus, displaying the trophy, posing for selfies and soaking up the fans' love and affection.

Next, they flew to Durban, where the crowds showed the same support and enthusiasm. Then on to East London and an incredible day in Port Elizabeth, where the team visited Zwide, the sprawling township where Siya Kolisi was born and learned to play the game. The sight of Siya being embraced by his joyful fans was one Cheslin would always remember.

He was impatient to get to his own home town, Cape Town, the last stop on their tour. He looked forward to driving down familiar streets and seeing the people he had been away from for so long.

The team arrived in Cape Town on Monday 11 November. It was a normal working day, but thousands of people came out into the streets to pay tribute to their heroes and to thank them for bringing pride and joy back to South Africans. Cheslin felt a lump in his throat as he looked down on the crowded streets and up at the famous Table Mountain in the background.

The last time the Springboks had won the Rugby World Cup, in 2007, Cheslin had been a young teenager. He had clear memories of watching the team celebrating their victory and over the years had wondered what it would feel like. To experience it now was overwhelming.

As the bus turned into Loop Street on the final leg of their tour, he saw a father hoisting his small son onto his shoulders so that the little boy could see better. The scene brought a very special memory back to Cheslin.

## CHAPTER 2

# *LEARNING FROM HIS FATHER*

It was late afternoon in Parow and six-year-old Cheslin was waiting impatiently in his dad's car outside the factory where he worked. The two of them were going to watch the Stormers play at Newlands but his dad was taking his time. Finally, Cheslin saw him shaking hands with a couple of colleagues and waving goodbye. He ran to the car, jumped in, and slammed the door shut.

'We're going to miss the fireworks show,' said Cheslin sadly.

'Sorry that took so long, my boy. People kept asking me for advice and I couldn't say no,' explained his dad.

'Are you the boss of all those people?'

'Not exactly, Chessie. But I know a thing or two,' he replied as he swung their old car into the traffic heading for town. 'And here's something else I know: if we beat the Highlanders tonight, we're definitely celebrating!'

'Ice cream?' asked Cheslin.

His dad nodded and laughed. 'Piles of the stuff!' he shouted and turned up the radio loud.

Cheslin settled back in his seat and watched as Table Mountain got closer and his dad talked non-stop about the upcoming game. He loved nothing more than hanging out with his dad and discussing a game or playing touch rugby with him in the streets.

Sometimes Cheslin would accompany his father to watch him play for Hands and Hearts, a rugby team that represented Kraaifontein in the local amateur divisions. Occasionally, during training, the Hands and Hearts players would let Cheslin join in, making him feel like he was part of the team.

Cheslin knew every player on the Stormers team, and their strengths and weaknesses. He knew more about rugby than anyone else did in his class – maybe even in the whole school.

Finally arriving in Newlands, his dad parked on the field at Groote Schuur High School, and they rushed towards the stadium. They heard the roar of the crowd – the game had started. Cheslin's dad swept his son up, placed him on his shoulders, and broke into a run.

Then they were through the gates and making their way up the steep stairs, squinting at the field against the bright sun. It was 1999, and that year the Stormers were enjoying a successful Super 12 season. They had only lost three games and had qualified to play in the semi-final against New Zealand's Otago Highlanders.

Cheslin could not contain his excitement about being at such an important game, and when Breyton Paulse found some space to cut through the defence and score, Cheslin was up on his feet and screaming. Breyton was his hero that season and this was one of the player's finest moments.

But no matter how hard they tried, the Stormers were outplayed, losing the game with a score of 18 points to 33. As they filed out of the stadium, the crowd was subdued. Everyone just wanted to get home. Cheslin was equally disappointed, but his earlier idea was still on his mind.

'Dad?' he asked. 'Maybe we can still get ice cream, because the team did make it all the way to the semi-final?'

His dad stopped, knelt down and put his hand on Cheslin's shoulder. 'You know what? That's the best idea I've heard all day. Let's celebrate making it to the semi-final!' he said.

'And next year, we'll go all the way to the finals!' Cheslin beamed.

## CHAPTER 3

# *DISCOVERING HIS SPEED*

On sports day, the Kolbe family lined up alongside the running track to watch the 100 metres final that Cheslin was competing in. The whole afternoon had been fun in the sun with their friends and neighbours, all of whom had children at Simonsberg Primary School in Kraaifontein.

The high jump, long jump and other field events were over, and now it was time for the track races to begin. There was no doubt that the 100 metres race was the most exciting event and everyone gathered around to watch.

From the corner of his eye, Andrew, Cheslin's dad, spotted his son lining up to start the next race. But that couldn't be right, Andrew thought. Cheslin was in Grade 4, but he was lining up with the Grades 5 and 6 boys.

'Wait, what's going on? That's not his age

group,' he muttered.

'Maybe Cheslin's so excited to run that he can't wait to get going, even in the wrong race,' laughed a nearby parent.

At that moment, Andrew spotted a teacher he knew, who was walking past. He stopped her and asked why Cheslin was crouching down, ready to run.

'Oh, don't worry, it's the right race. The Grade 4s didn't want to race with him. They said it was unfair.'

'But … what … why? I don't understand,' Andrew stuttered, even more confused.

'Just wait, you'll see,' the teacher grinned.

Andrew shrugged and thought about how to comfort his son later, after losing the race. Cheslin had talked about nothing but the 100-metres race for days, so it was going to be a huge disappointment for him. Frowning, he reached down, pulled a sandwich out of the cooler box at his feet and took a big bite just as the whistle blew for the start of the race.

Andrew's jaw clamped shut in surprise, and

he almost choked on the sandwich as he watched Cheslin pull away swiftly and hold first position the entire race. Only moments after it had begun, the race was over, with almost ten metres between Cheslin and the other boys fighting for second place.

The crowd was cheering and laughing as they gathered around Cheslin to slap him on the back and congratulate him. Of course, Andrew knew his son was a fast runner, but he had no idea he was this fast, easily competing against boys who were older than him.

Cheslin came running over to his dad, who gave him a bear hug.

'Well done, my boy, that was just … sensational!'

'Thanks, Dad.'

Cheslin was thrilled with all the attention and with how well the race had gone. He loved to compete and of course he loved to win. But mostly he just loved the feeling of going at full speed. It felt almost like he was flying on his own two legs.

★★★

For a few weeks now, Cheslin had been cooped up at home, and he was frustrated. Gangsterism and crime were getting worse in Scottsville, a section of Kraaifontein, and none of the parents in his street felt that it was safe to let their children play outside. So Cheslin had to spend most of his free time inside, watching television, reading comic books, or doing whatever he could to keep himself occupied.

When he was allowed out to play, Cheslin made the most of it. There was always a game of soccer, cricket or rugby to join and he played with his heart and soul, as though he was participating in a World Cup final. It was not unusual for him to start a game in the bright daylight and to continue playing when the streetlights came on.

The Van Niekerks, Cheslin's relatives, lived quite close by and the two families often spent time together. His cousin, Wayde, who was about the same age as him, was also a fast runner and keen on sports.

The adults in the family enjoyed watching them racing against each other, but Cheslin preferred it when he and Wayde were on the same team. Then they could run rings around the other boys.

A couple of boys down the road, the Van Staden brothers, had the reputation of being the roughest in the area. They seemed not to understand the concept of touch rugby and did their best to crash into the other youngsters as often as possible. Their only goal was to prove how tough they were.

During one game, the Van Staden brothers were crashing into the players as usual, knocking them over and laughing. Late in the game, Wayde got the ball and dodged past one outstretched hand, then another and another. Both Van Staden boys ran towards him, and Cheslin saw they were going to try and sandwich Wayde between them.

He was worried about his cousin – but he did not need to be.

Wayde saw the brothers coming and, as they

reached out for him, he accelerated through the gap, then turned and watched as they crashed into each other and went tumbling to the ground. Everyone in the street burst out laughing and clapped loudly as Wayde ran the last few metres and dotted the ball down.

'Good one, Wayde', said Cheslin, running over and holding out his hand for a high-five. 'But you do know they'll be wanting revenge, don't you?'

Wayde shrugged. 'I'm not bothered. Those two will never catch me – or you, for that matter.'

'When did you get so quick?'

'I don't know. Every day I try to go just a little bit faster.'

'Sounds good. Race you back home?'

'Bad idea, cuz. But OK; if you don't mind being a loser.'

'On your marks, get set, go!' said Wayde, and raced off, closely followed by Cheslin, who was laughing and whooping as he chased. The boys ran freely through the streets as the

As kids, Cheslin and Wayde went everywhere together at full speed.

orange sunset glowed behind a distant Table Mountain. They could not imagine life getting any better.

## CHAPTER 4

# *SCHOOL DAYS*

The year was 2005 and Cheslin was in Grade 6 at Simonsberg Primary School. It was his and Wayde's first rugby practice and they felt super excited as they walked out of the school buildings in their rugby togs. Mr Field had told the team to expect a special guest.

On the field, the coach was telling the team to sit in a semi-circle. They took their places and sat. A short while later, Wayde pointed to a man getting out of a car in the nearby parking lot, dressed in a Springbok tracksuit and holding a rugby ball in his hands.

As the man walked closer, Cheslin recognised his face. 'No ways,' he said. 'That's ... Adrian Jacobs.'

Jacobs had grown up in Kraaifontein and had made his Springbok debut against Italy in

2001. That game had gone well, but his second game a year later was disastrous: England defeated South Africa by a whopping 53 points to three. Since then, Adrian had not been called up to play for the Springbok team, but people speculated it was only a matter of time.

Wayde and Cheslin listened closely as Jacobs described how hard he was working to get back into the Springbok team and what his training was like. He also told the boys about growing up in the early nineties, and how at school he had been told, time after time, that he was too small and weak to become a Springbok.

'If you really want to play rugby,' Jacobs said, 'my advice to you is to ignore haters and critics, and fight to the end in every game that you play.'

Cheslin felt as though Jacobs was talking directly to him.

After the talk was over, the team got up and sprinted off to warm up while their coach spoke to Jacobs, but Cheslin and Wayde hung back.

Mr Field looked up and saw them waiting.

'Cheslin, come and meet Adrian Jacobs.'

Jacobs bent down and they shook hands.

'He's the one I was telling you about,' said Mr Field and the Springbok player nodded.

'What position do you play?' Jacobs asked Cheslin.

'Anywhere in the back line,' he replied.

'He's going to be left wing for the Springboks,' said Wayde, 'and I'm going to be right wing.'

'Why not?' laughed Jacobs. 'I can see that happening.'

Cheslin felt thrilled but he had a burning question that he needed to ask.

'I was wondering … when did you have your biggest growth spurt?'

'Um … I can't remember, really. Why do you ask?'

'I'm still too small for the team. At least, that's what everyone keeps telling me, but … I don't know.'

'Too small? Doesn't look like it to me,' said Jacobs. 'You look light on your feet, as if you could fly straight up into the air.'

'I can.'

Jacobs grinned at him. 'Lemme tell you a secret, Cheslin. One small guy to another. Come here.'

Cheslin came in close as Jacobs whispered, 'If the big guys can't catch you, then the big guys can't hurt you.'

Cheslin grinned back. 'They'll never catch me,' he said.

'Good ... there's no right size for any position on the rugby field. I've played against big and small, and trust me, it's the little guys you have to watch out for.'

Cheslin nodded. He understood exactly what Jacobs was telling him.

Jacobs picked up a ball and took a few steps back, holding it in one hand, like an American quarterback.

'Go long!' he shouted, and the rest of the team stopped what they were doing and turned to watch. 'Where's my wide receiver?' Jacobs looked around, pretending to dodge an attacker.

Cheslin and Wayde sprang into action, running fast away from Jacobs, while turning to watch as he threw the ball hard and high towards them. The boys each adjusted their path instinctively, sped up and then jumped to receive the ball – but Cheslin, who was just centimetres in front, got to it first. He pulled it down, protecting it as he landed, then darted left and spun right before he ran towards his teammates and dived high with the ball over the line to score a beautiful try right under the posts.

'Touchdown!' he shouted, and the whole team cheered.

Jacobs ran over and shook Cheslin's hand. 'Nice moves, kid. I think we're getting our rugby and American football moves mixed up, but it's all good!'

Wayde gave him a high-five. 'Nice catch, Ches. I almost had it.'

'So, what's your surname, Cheslin?' asked Jacobs.

'Kolbe. Cheslin Kolbe.'

'Cool. Nice to meet you. That pass you

caught … that was me passing the Springbok torch on to you, Cheslin Kolbe.'

# CHAPTER 5

# *LEARNING THE SIDESTEP*

Simonsberg Primary had a good season, winning some of the big games against school teams from all over Cape Town. They were learning how to play together and had built a strong team spirit.

Cheslin and Wayde and their families had become even closer. Now that they were in the same team, the boys saw each other often and the extended family met up at the games.

The last game of the season was against one of the strongest teams in the area, Brackenfell Primary. But Simonsberg was undefeated that season and the team was determined that it should stay that way.

'You know who plays for them, right?' Wayde asked Cheslin, the day before the game.

'It doesn't matter, and I don't care. We've got this,' Cheslin answered.

'*Ja*, but this is different. Those Van Staden brothers are both in the team. One plays lock and the other plays eighth man. You know they won't be happy till they've rubbed our faces in the dirt in front of the whole school.'

'Hmm … That's true,' said Cheslin, falling silent. Wayde could see that he was thinking about an idea.

Suddenly Cheslin bounced up. 'Let's go outside. There's this move I saw on TV that I've been wanting to practise.'

★★★

The next day, a light rain fell, and the wind was gathering speed as the opposing teams lined up for the final match of the season. Cheslin bounced around, trying to keep warm until the game started.

He was delighted to see his dad's car pulling up outside the school just as the referee fetched the ball and placed it. Kolbe senior jumped out of the car and ran towards the school gate. They had a running joke that he was late for every game, but he insisted that he was always

29

there for the opening whistle.

As the referee blew the whistle, he saw his dad punch a fist into the air, celebrating that he had made it there on time.

'Come on Cheslin! Come on Simonsberg! Let's go, boys!' his dad shouted from the sideline as the game kicked off.

Within the first few minutes, it became clear that this was not going to be an easy victory. Their opponents were well coached and well organised, and they had a skilled flyhalf who kept the ball alive for the backline.

Cheslin spent most of the first half on defence – tackling, getting up and tackling again. Wayde had been right about the Van Staden boys. They were clearly enjoying the pressure they were putting on the defence, and they were following it up with a lot of chatter and insults, especially towards Wayde and Cheslin.

When the half-time whistle blew, the score was 12 points to three and Simonsberg Primary was facing its first big defeat.

Mr Field called the boys together and tried to boost their confidence. 'You're doing fine, guys, really you are. They've had a few lucky breaks but all we have to do is score early in the second half and then we're back in the game. No doubt!'

Cheslin nodded as he sucked on a piece of orange and rubbed a sore calf muscle.

Wayde came over to him. 'Remember that new move we were practising? This is the perfect time to try it out. I'll get the ball to you when we're on the halfway line and you run at Anton van Staden and do that "thing".'

'You think so?'

'Definitely, Ches. It's the last game of the season, man. You'll be a legend.'

'OK, I'll do it. We're probably going to lose anyway, so why not?'

The game kicked off again and the pattern resumed. The other team surged forward and began a slow march towards the try line. Then an interception suddenly changed the direction of play. Wayde picked up the ball, looked for

Cheslin on the wing and threw a long skip pass that sailed over the inside centres and into Cheslin's arms.

Cheslin knew this was the moment. Instead of trying to run around the outside edge of the defenders, he headed straight for the pack. Anton saw Cheslin coming and a sly smile crossed his lips.

Cheslin, who was watching him closely, decided to go left. He shortened his stride and checked his balance, then stepped onto his right leg and shifted his weight as if he was going that way. Anton fell for it completely and lifted his beefy arms.

That was the signal Cheslin was waiting for and he immediately exploded off his right leg and onto the left, accelerating past Anton, who was still going the other way. After that, it was a straight jog over towards the line where he dotted down for the try.

Moments later, the other Van Staden boy crashed into Cheslin, sending him flying. 'Oh sorry, I didn't see you there, little guy!' he sneered.

Cheslin bounced angrily to his feet. 'What the heck, bro?' he shouted.

Wayde appeared within seconds and he was even more furious. 'What do you think you're doing, Van Staden?'

For a few seconds, all four of them stood there, ready to fight but the referee blew hard on his whistle and separated them.

'You OK?' asked Wayde.

'Sure. No problem. How was the sidestep?'

'Dude … You are officially a master. That was a thing of beauty,' Wayde said as they jogged back and waited for the conversion kick.

'Master of the sidestep,' Cheslin said to himself as the game restarted. 'I think I could get used to that.'

★★★

Cheslin's confidence on the field kept growing. He was regularly selected for the school rugby team and he also became a star on the athletics track. He had a real passion for hurdles. There was something about the rhythm of running and jumping that suited him. He was shorter

Cheslin had a real passion for hurdles.

than most of the other hurdlers, but he had a spring in his step that lifted him over every time.

After winning every hurdles race that he entered that season, Cheslin was selected for the Western Province athletics squad. Even though it did not come as much of a surprise to anyone, Cheslin felt extremely pleased to have been noticed as a top athlete.

Things were going well and Cheslin was looking forward to high school the following year, although he worried about how his parents were going to pay the fees. Times were tough and they were struggling to make ends meet.

One morning in early August, Cheslin and his dad visited Brackenfell High School, where they had an appointment to meet with the sports head teacher, Mr Stofberg. They walked through the parking lot together and then into the reception area.

They did not have to wait for long before the teacher appeared, greeted them warmly and led them to an office down the passage.

As soon as Cheslin shook Mr Stofberg's hand, he felt sure that the teacher was a warm, kind and caring man.

First, they spoke about the academic curriculum. The school offered all subjects in both English and Afrikaans, and Cheslin said that he would prefer to be taught in English. Then the talk turned to sport, and Cheslin sat up straighter in his chair.

'You know we have an excellent athletics programme at this school, don't you? We take the sport very seriously,' Mr Stofberg said.

'Yes, sir,' said Cheslin.

'And we've been following your progress on the track. It's impressive.'

'Thank you, sir.'

'That's one of the reasons we want you at our school, and we're prepared to offer you an athletics scholarship to help with the fees.'

Cheslin's jaw fell open and he turned to look at his dad, who sat smiling beside him.

'That's very kind of you, Mr Stofberg. Thank you,' his dad said, patting Cheslin on the back.

'Hopefully, you can bring all that speed to the rugby field, too, Cheslin,' said Mr Stofberg, showing them to the door. 'We need good players in our backline.'

As they left the school building, Cheslin turned excitedly to his dad.

'Can I please come here, Dad? I like this school.'

'I like it too. I think it's decided.'

# CHAPTER 6

## *HANDLING HIGH SCHOOL*

Along with all Cheslin's excitement about high school there was some sadness, too. Wayde's parents were getting divorced and Wayde was moving to Bloemfontein with his mother and stepfather.

'I don't know a single person there,' complained Wayde one day.

'You'll make friends quickly,' said Cheslin, trying to reassure him.

'D'you think they do athletics there?'

'Of course, man. You'll be the star of the show.'

Wayde nodded and carried on aiming stones at the lamppost on the other side of the road. Worry was etched all over his face.

'Remember our plan to play first-team rugby together? That's not going to happen now.'

'I guess not,' said Cheslin. 'We'll just have to wait until we both become Stormers players. Then we'll show everyone.'

Wayde pulled his arm back and was about to throw the ball, but suddenly stopped. 'Oh no! I just realised …'

'What?' asked Cheslin, concerned.

'The guys in my new school. They're going to expect me to become a Cheetahs fan, aren't they?' Wayde laughed bitterly.

'OK, this is too much,' said Cheslin, trying to seem serious. 'Listen to me, Wayde. If you become a Cheetahs fan, don't bother coming back here. Ever.'

'Don't worry, Ches. That's never going to happen. Stormers are in my blood.'

A few days later, the Kolbe family helped the Van Niekerks load the last few items into their car and waved them goodbye as they set off on their long journey to the Free State. Cheslin felt lonely and anxious for Wayde at first, but after he chatted to his cousin on the phone and heard that he was doing OK, his mind turned to the excitement of becoming a Grade 8 high-school student.

★★★

Brackenfell High School – affectionately known as Brakkies – was big and busy. There was a lot for Cheslin to get used to. Hundreds of students poured through the gates every morning and for a while he felt as though he would never figure out where he was supposed to be, and at what time.

In the rugby team, the important thing was boots. Everyone seemed to be obsessed with them. At primary school, Cheslin's team and most other teams had played rugby barefoot. Very occasionally, they would play against a Southern Suburbs team who wore boots. But now everyone was talking about boots all the time.

Cheslin's parents wanted him to feel part of the team, so they bought him a pair. Those boots gave him fresh confidence. He was unafraid to go in for some tough tackles now that his feet were protected. Wearing them, he felt unstoppable.

But sometimes, Cheslin could not help laughing as he stood at the backline, waiting for a pass after a scrum, and the game ground to a halt while players wiped dirt and mud off their shiny new boots – causing the coach to scream at them in frustration and anger.

Something he had not expected to find at Brackenfell High School was the Van Staden brothers, and it was a nasty shock to hear their familiar, taunting voices behind him on the first day.

'Hey shorty! Are you sure you're ready for high school?'

'Jeepers! When are you planning to grow a bit, Kolbe?'

And they both doubled up, cackling at their own stupid jokes.

Cheslin tried not to let it show but secretly he did worry that he would never grow taller. Why was he so slow to grow, when the boys around him seemed to add on centimetres every day? Nevertheless, he was determined to compete with boys twice his size – and to win.

Sevens rugby was a happy high-school discovery for Cheslin. The game seemed to be created for him. It required speed, fitness and skill, and Cheslin ticked all those boxes. People started to notice the little guy with the fast feet. He was a natural at the game and it was love at first sight.

★★★

Under the guidance of the Brackenfell coaching staff, Cheslin's rugby skills were going from strength to strength. Everything improved – his handling of the ball, his sidestep, acceleration. Sometimes it seemed he was able to score points whenever he felt like it.

Mr Stofberg told Andrew that the way his son read the game was unusual.

'It's almost like he's looking down at the game from above and can see things happening that the rest of the players just can't see.'

'He's always been like that,' said Andrew. 'Since he was a small kid.'

Cheslin was also excelling at athletics, but something about being part of a winning team appealed more to him. Out on the track, staring down the hurdles, he was all alone; but when he was on the rugby field he knew there were 14 other players who would do anything for him in the moment, just like he would do anything for them. That was a good feeling to have.

When he started playing at under-16 level, his thoughts turned to the most important annual inter-provincial school rugby tournament in the country – Grant Khomo Week. It was a rugby player's first chance to get noticed by professional teams.

Cheslin desperately wanted to be selected for the Western Province team and to test himself against players from other provinces. But there was a problem: he would be judged against players from Paul Roos and Paarl Gym who had been training for this since they first pulled on rugby boots in primary school. He thought he could do it, but Mr Stofberg was realistic about his chances.

'Sorry to say, Ches, but if it's between you and them, they're going to get picked. It's not just about talent; the selectors have been following their progress for years. That's just how it is with the bigger schools.'

Cheslin was disappointed but Mr Stofberg had a suggestion.

'For the trials that are coming up, here's what I think we should do. Next game, instead of playing centre, I think you should start at flyhalf. If you do well, then you've got a better chance of making the team in that position.'

Cheslin did not hesitate for a second. 'No problem, coach. I'm ready to play flyhalf.'

So, on the team sheet for the first game of the trials, Cheslin's name appeared under flyhalf. But on the way to the game, Mr Stofberg noticed that he was unusually quiet.

'What is it, Ches?' asked the coach.

'Thing is … I've never played flyhalf before. I'm not exactly sure I know how to.'

Mr Stofberg laughed. 'Of course you do. You've played alongside flyhalf your whole career. Now you just have to be one.'

'OK, but I don't want to let the team down.'

The coach could see that Cheslin was worried. 'OK listen to me, this is the plan. Everyone knows you can score tries; everyone knows you can break the line. That's not what they're looking for. They want to see whether you can distribute the ball to your backline, how you keep it alive, how much of a team player you are. Think you can do that?'

'So, no scoring on my own?'

The coach paused. 'One try only.'

'And no line breaks?'

'One in the first half. One in the second. Otherwise, your job is to make the others look good.'

'Got it, Coach.'

There were so many trial games scheduled for that day that Mr Stofberg was called from one place to the next, and he missed Cheslin's game. The coach had to wait until they were on the bus home to find out how it went.

'No problem, Coach,' replied Cheslin. 'One try, two line breaks, and lots of good passing. Just like you ordered.'

Mr Stofberg laughed and gave him a high five. A few days later, the coach was not at all surprised to see Cheslin's name included in the under-16 Grant Khomo team for Western Province.

That call up to the Western Province team in 2009 changed Cheslin's life in two ways.

First, he got a taste of being a player at Newlands, rather than a spectator. To be in the same changerooms and walk down the same tunnel and onto the same grass as his heroes was truly special. He felt as though just being there improved his game.

Second, Brackenfell High School gave him a rugby scholarship as a reward. This, together with the athletics scholarship, covered his full school fees, so his parents no longer had to worry. He was proud to be able to help his family financially.

If there was any doubt that Cheslin had a future as a professional sportsman, being selected for the Western Province team put that to rest. He could feel he was good enough, and

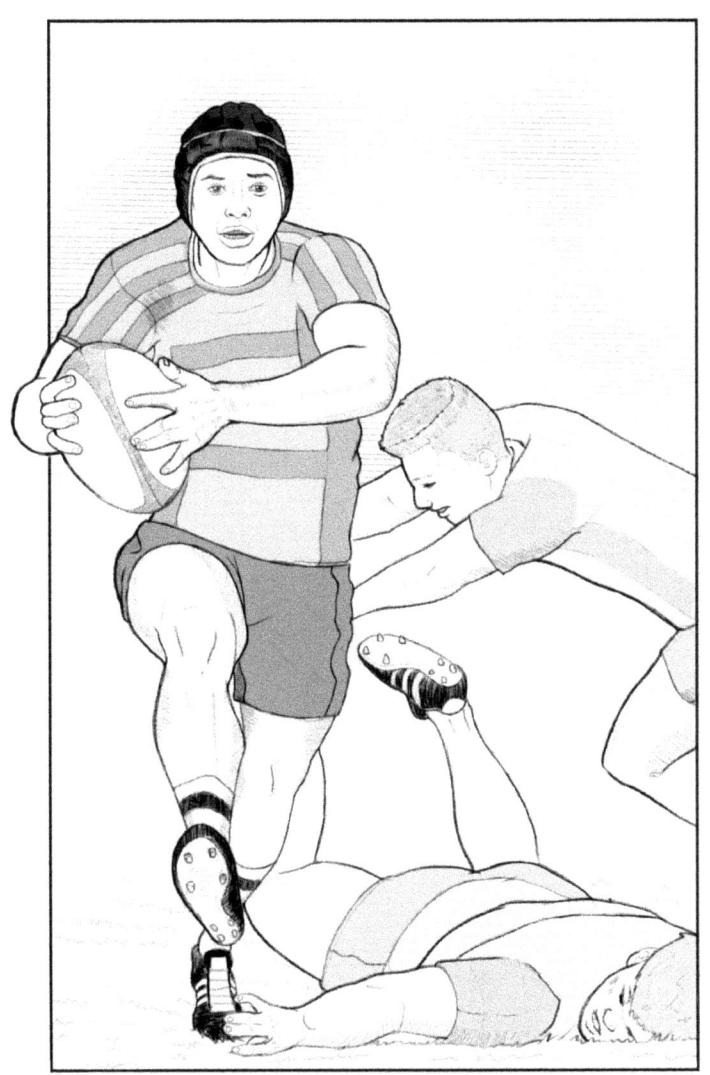

Breaking tackles and perfecting his sidestep? All in a day's work.

it made him even more determined to be the best he could be.

# CHAPTER 7

## *TIME TO MOVE ON?*

The rumour started going round school at the beginning of term. Nobody knew who said it first, but soon everyone took it as a fact that Cheslin would be leaving Brakkies and going to one of the big rugby schools.

Some people were upset, others were happy for him; but few questioned whether it was true. When Mr Stofberg heard the story, he refused to discuss it.

'I'll believe it when I hear it from Cheslin himself. Until then, it's just a rumour.'

For a few days he heard nothing, but then the headmaster came to tell him that Andrew Kolbe had called to make an appointment.

'I guess this is it then,' the coach muttered, and the headmaster shrugged.

It was true that Cheslin had been approached

by Bishops and Paarl Boys' High, and both schools had offered him a scholarship – as well as free kit and other perks – in their effort to get him to switch schools. He had even taken part in a training session at Paarl Boys' High to see what it was like.

What did Cheslin feel about all of this? Truth be told, he was having mixed feelings. He felt honoured and excited, but at the same time something did not feel right, and it was keeping him up at night. How was he going to make the best choice to secure his future?

Eventually, the whole family got together to discuss what to do. Even his older sister came over to see if she could help. After plenty of discussion, they came to a decision.

The next morning Cheslin and his dad arrived at the school together.

'You sure you don't want to come with me to speak to Coach?' Andrew asked his son.

Cheslin nodded. 'You've got this, Dad. And I can't afford to miss the maths test this morning.'

'OK, son. I'll let you know how it goes.'

Cheslin ran off to class and Andrew went into the school's reception area to wait for Mr Stofberg.

In the coach's office, the two men first talked about South Africa winning the recent British and Irish Lions Test series before falling into an uneasy silence.

'So …' said Mr Stofberg.

'I'm sure you've heard the rumours by now,' said Andrew, and Mr Stofberg nodded.

'You've been really good to us, Mr Stofberg, and so has this school. We're extremely appreciative of what you've done for Cheslin.'

Mr Stofberg nodded, and Andrew could see from his expression that he was expecting bad news.

'That's why we've decided to stay. We want Cheslin to complete his schooling here at Brackenfell High.'

'What? Are you sure?' the coach asked him.

'Quite sure. You took a chance on my boy when other schools were not interested, and we value that. Loyalty is important to us.'

A delighted Mr Stofberg thumped the desk happily.

'That's fantastic news and I promise, you won't regret it,' he said, standing up and shaking Mr Kolbe's hand. 'Thank you.'

As soon as the two men parted, Mr Stofberg rushed off to tell the headmaster the good news.

★★★

Cheslin's interest in hurdles began fading. He still participated in athletics during the season, but his heart was not in it. However, his dedication to rugby was rewarded with captaincy of the First XV and he took his leadership role seriously.

Cheslin spent as much time as possible on the field. When an injury kept him out of a game, he paced impatiently up and down the sideline. At one of these times, watching a game against Tygerberg High School, Cheslin could no longer contain his frustration. Brackenfell was 20 points down at half-time, and he felt certain that he could turn the game around.

Mr Stofberg was not in favour of this approach.

'Stay off the field and look after your health,' he told Cheslin. 'That's what really counts.'

But a few minutes later, there was a roar from the crowd. Cheslin had snuck away and put on his kit and was ready to play. Shaking his head, Mr Stofberg allowed him into the game.

Sure enough, Cheslin's presence on the field changed everything. He was dynamite – breaking the line and charging forward when he could, then defending like a demon when the other side attacked. As the minutes ticked by, the advantage swung back to Brackenfell and they won the game.

During Cheslin's matric year, he was selected to join Western Province's under-18 team for the 2011 Craven Week. He would play alongside other talented upcoming rugby players, most of whom were from Paarl Gimnasium, Paarl Boys' High and Paul Roos. The tournament was scheduled to take place in Welkom and Cheslin felt sad that his family could not be there.

But he was mistaken.

'You think I'm going to miss your Craven

Week debut?' his dad said indignantly. 'Are you crazy?'

So that winter, the Kolbe family bundled into their car and made the long trip inland to Welkom to watch the finest schoolboy rugby players in South Africa compete. Some of the most talented were Handré Pollard and Sikhumbuzo Notshe from Western Province, Lood de Jager from Eastern Province, and RJ van Rensburg who played for Pretoria's Blue Bulls team. Despite the fierce competition, Cheslin was determined to shine.

A nice surprise on the first day of the tournament was seeing Adrian Jacobs again. Cheslin had last seen him on the rugby field at Simonsberg Primary School, when the player had been dropped from the Springboks, after a disastrous defeat to England.

It had taken Jacobs seven seasons to earn another call-up for the Boks, but he had done it. Now he was an outside centre for the national team, alongside Jean de Villiers. He had come to help the Springbok talent scouts identify key players at the tournament.

'Cheslin!' he shouted, moments before the first game. 'When I saw the team line-up earlier, I wondered if that was you. Remember me?'

'Are you joking? Of course I remember you. It's wild that you remember me.'

Jacobs laughed. 'I'm glad to see you didn't stop playing. What happened to your cousin?'

'Wayde? Oh, he's doing great. Athletics is his thing now.'

'That's cool. Looking forward to seeing you play,' Jacobs shouted as the teams ran onto the field.

But despite their best efforts, the Western Province boys had a difficult Craven Week, winning only one of their three games and missing out on the finals.

However, Cheslin's disappointment did not last long. Soon after the team returned home, he found out that he had been selected for the South African rugby sevens team that would participate in the Commonwealth Youth Games in September, in the Isle of Man.

Rugby sevens was growing in popularity throughout the world. Brackenfell High had an excellent sevens team and Cheslin loved the game as much as he loved playing regular rugby. To be selected to represent his country at the Commonwealth Youth Games meant he really did have a future in the sport.

'The Isle of Man? That's on the other side of the world,' said his dad when he heard the news. 'I'm afraid that's one game we're not going to be able to attend, Cheslin.'

★★★

At the Games, South Africa was placed in Group B alongside England, Sri Lanka and Trinidad and Tobago. They cruised easily past Trinidad and Tobago but faced a tougher match against England and ended up losing it, with a score of five points to seven.

On the second day of the competition, they came back strongly against Canada, winning by 24 points to 12, which earned them the silver medal overall, behind England. It was an awesome experience for Cheslin, who thoroughly enjoyed touring the island and being part of an international team.

However, it was also his matric year, so schoolwork was never far from his mind. Being good at rugby was no excuse for failing in the classroom and his parents had always insisted that he keep his marks up.

He was concentrating hard on a maths problem when the phone call came. It was the SAS Rugby Sevens Academy in Stellenbosch, inviting him to be part of their training programme after he matriculated. There, he would receive first-class coaching and medical care, as well as a small salary. His journey towards becoming an international rugby player had started.

'Dad! Listen to this!' he screamed as soon as he had digested the news. 'They want me to turn pro. To play sevens full time. It's my dream come true!'

'You've earned it, Ches. You've earned it,' was all his choked-up father could say in return.

On the last day of exams, Cheslin put down

his pen, knowing that he had done his best, and ready to celebrate with his school friends and teammates. He said an emotional farewell to Mr Stofberg, but he knew it was not a final goodbye. The administrators of Western Province Rugby had noticed the coach's talents and had selected him to be part of their administrative staff, so Cheslin would continue to see a lot of him.

Looking back, Cheslin was proud of his decision to stay at Brackenfell and grateful for their support. He knew his time there had set him up for an exciting future.

CHAPTER 8

# *TURNING PRO*

Driving out to Stellenbosch to take up his place in the Sevens Academy was a big moment for Cheslin. It was 2012, and he was starting a new, independent life as a professional sportsman.

He thought about the hundreds of games he had played, the hours spent running, tackling and practising. Now he was going to be paid to do what he had always done happily for free.

The academy in Stellenbosch was a beautiful setup. Each player's room led onto a court-yard surrounding a blue lap pool. There were high-tech training and medical facilities, and world-class coaches to help the players get to the next level.

Cheslin was raring to go and surprised to discover that the players would not be touching a ball for the first few days. Instead, the focus was on medical checks and fitness. The physio-therapists had realised that many players carry old injuries, and these problems needed to be cleared up before the season kicked off.

For several years, Cheslin had been having shoulder issues. Now was the perfect time to get this sorted out. So he had a small operation which meant it was a few weeks before he could play at full contact again.

The programme at the academy was tough. Most mornings, the players were on the field by 6 am and trained until breakfast at 7.30 am. At 9 am there was an injury report and squad meeting, followed by another training and coaching session until 12.30 pm.

In the early afternoon, the players did physio-therapy or relaxed, then they gathered again for the final training session from 4 to 5 pm. Although it felt gruelling at times, Cheslin enjoyed the programme and he was amazed at how quickly his skills and fitness level improved.

From January until May, the academy players worked with the same goal in mind – to join the Western Province squad for the second half of the season. Cheslin felt nervous in the days leading up to the selection, but he was confident that he had worked hard. And the hard work paid off. He was chosen for the Western Province under-21 squad, coached by John Dobson.

The team learned that they would play in the ABSA Under-21 Provincial Championship, from July to October, against teams like the Blue Bulls, Sharks and Golden Lions. Cheslin relished his first opportunity to be part of a professional touring club and to play in inter-national standard rugby stadiums. Ellis Park one week, Newlands the next, then moving on to Kings Park in Durban and Free State Stadium – it was a wonderful way to get used to the travel and excitement of being a touring professional.

The team worked hard, winning eight of their 12 games, and finishing third in Division A, which meant they qualified for the semi-finals against the Sharks at Kings Park Stadium. In a heart-stopping, close game, the visiting

Western Province team managed to squeeze past the Sharks, winning by 19 points to 18.

The final between Blue Bulls and Western Province took place on neutral territory at Kings Park on 27 October. Dobson decided to put his faith in six of the team's under-20 players, and so Cheslin experienced his first cup final game. But the Bulls were simply too strong, and they won the Championship 22 points to 13. For Western Province, it was a disappointing end to a great season.

Things seemed to go much more smoothly at the start of the second season. Cheslin was accustomed to the setup at the academy, he understood the systems in place at Western Province and he was feeling confident in his game.

It was rapidly shaping up to be a busy year. The first serious tournament was the 2013 Vodacom Cup, which took place from March to May. Western Province finished second in their group behind the Sharks. Out of the seven games, they won five, drew one and lost one.

In the quarter-finals, they were drawn to

play against Griquas at Newlands. The game attracted only a small crowd, but still the players put in maximum effort. Griquas scored first, with a try and conversion in the 35th minute. Everyone expected them to go into the half-time break with Griquas leading seven points to nil, but moments before the whistle blew Cheslin scored a try that evened out the points.

After the break, Cheslin was standing on the halfway line when the Griquas flyhalf put in a massive kick, sending the ball over everyone's heads and into Cheslin's arms. He looked up, mentally seeing a path that led all the way to the posts. He swerved past one defender, threw off another and broke a third tackle. Then there was some space and he accelerated through it before a final sidestep left a fourth defender grasping at fresh air.

Cheslin dived over the line. He had run all alone from the halfway line and had outclassed every defender on the field. The Western Province coach, John Dobson, who was standing on the touchline, was speechless – a few years later, he would remark that this was the best individual try that he had seen in his whole career.

'If you were a trader on the stock exchange, you'd buy shares in Cheslin Kolbe, and you'd become very wealthy,' said Dobson to the press after the game.

## CHAPTER 9

# *GOOD THINGS KEEP HAPPENING*

The Western Province senior management followed Cheslin's progress carefully. They decided to reward him with a place on the Stormers bench during the Super 14. Just to pull on a Stormers jersey and run out on the field with the senior team was more than he had hoped for, and he did not expect to get into a game.

Even though he was not on the field, he knew that his parents were proudly watching him from the stands – probably sitting exactly where he and his dad used to sit all those years ago.

Good things kept happening. A few weeks later, he was selected for the Springbok under-20 squad that was set to go to France. They would be defending the title they had won the previous year, when they beat the All Blacks by 22 points to 16 in the final of the

2012 International Rugby Board Junior World Championship.

Cheslin had become good friends with Justin Geduld, who was at the academy and a Western Province player. Justin had also made the squad and they sat together on the plane.

'Remember when Stellenbosch seemed far from home?' said Cheslin. 'Now look at us.'

'Remember when playing at Newlands was our biggest dream?' replied Justin. 'Now we're off to an Under-20 World Cup in France.'

'And this is just the beginning. We're not stopping until we're holding up the Webb Ellis trophy in the senior World Cup,' said Cheslin and they high-fived as the plane rushed over the Atlantic Ocean on its way to Europe.

When Cheslin looked back at his childhood fears — about being too small, about never having the growth spurt that he needed — they seemed so unimportant. Now he believed that all he had to do was stay fit and healthy and God's plan for him would unfold.

The South Africans won all three of their

pool games in the Under-20 World Cup, beating the United States, England and France. The game against the hosts was a close one. The Springboks were only leading by two points when Cheslin scored a beautiful try just before the final whistle, slotting into the backline between the two centres around the 22-metre line, beating his marker and diving over into the corner to score.

With a final score of 26 points to 19, South Africa was in the playoffs. After the match, Cheslin was stopped by Olivier Roumat, a legendary French player. Roumat had played 61 times for his country and had also spent a season playing for the Sharks team that won the Currie Cup in 1995.

'That was excellent, Cheslin,' he said. 'Well done.'

'Oh, thanks a lot, sir.'

'You should think about playing your club rugby in France one day. Our system would suit a guy like you.'

'Really? I always heard that French teams

only picked the biggest players. In case you hadn't noticed, I'm not that guy,' joked Cheslin.

'That is just a stereotype. French rugby is changing all the time. Seriously, if it doesn't work out at home, get in touch.'

Cheslin's mind was soon on other things as the team prepared for their semi-final game against Wales in a beautiful, ancient town called Vannes. The game was extremely tight in the first half: two penalties to Wales and one converted try to South Africa gave the Junior Springboks a one-point lead.

During the second half, both teams scored tries but Wales missed their conversion and South Africa gained a three-point lead. Then another penalty made the score 17 points to 11 going into the last ten minutes, and South Africa began to look like they had it wrapped up.

But rugby is full of surprises. Fullback Jordan Williams made a superb break to put Wales onto the attack. Sam Davies set up a perfect chip that was caught by Ashley Evans, who crossed the line wide out on the wing.

All Wales needed was Sam Davies's fearless conversion to win the game in the dying seconds, with a one-point victory.

The South Africans felt crushed. Five minutes earlier the game had been theirs. But they managed to pick themselves up and wallop New Zealand a few days later, securing third place and a bronze medal.

There was no rest for Cheslin. From Paris he flew straight to Moscow, to join the Springbok team for the 2013 World Cup Sevens. It was such an honour to be part of that team, although he was disappointed to discover that the game was not popular in Russia and they were going to be playing in empty stadiums.

Still, exciting things seemed to be happening almost every day. The Stormers coach, Allister Coetzee, announced that Cheslin might be a potential replacement for Bryan Habana, whose career was coming to an end, and that Western Province was offering him a two-year extension on his contract.

'I wish we had time to play him in the final

three Super Rugby games,' said Coetzee. 'But he will probably have an opportunity to show us what he can do in the Currie Cup when he comes back from the World Cup Sevens. Yes, Cheslin will definitely be in the plans … he's a very exciting player.'

★★★

As predicted by Coetzee, Cheslin made his Currie Cup debut for Western Province in August 2013. The backline, with Gio Aplon, Juan de Jongh, Damian de Allende and Cheslin, was potent and lightning fast. Cheslin scored his first try for the team in a nail-biting draw against the Golden Lions at Ellis Park.

While Cheslin knew that he was playing well and contributing to the team, he was stunned to be named ABSA Currie Cup Player of the Month for August.

'It's a great moment for me to win this award,' he said afterwards. 'I didn't expect it, but I'll happily take it because I've worked hard in the competition thus far.'

The team were playing out of their skin.

They were undefeated during the regular season, drawing two and winning eight of their first ten matches and making it to the final.

On the morning of the final, Cheslin woke up with a knot in his stomach. He desperately wanted to do well, for himself, for his family and for Cape Town.

His dad reassured him. 'You've played huge games before. Remember when Paarl Boys' came to Brackenfell? It felt like the whole world was watching. Or playing for the Springboks sevens side? Same thing. When the whistle goes, it's the same game with the same rules.'

Cheslin nodded. He was grateful to have his dad's grounding influence in his life.

Later that day the two teams ran onto the pitch to line up for the national anthem, and the deafening roar of the crowd hit his ears like a roar of thunder. Cheslin tried to calm himself. The Currie Cup was the oldest professional rugby competition in the world and to win it meant everything to him.

Within six minutes of the start, the Province players were reeling. First a long penalty from Patrick Lambie gave the Sharks three points, then flyhalf Charl McLeod gathered the ball on the halfway line and ran all the way, chased by Damian de Allende, to score. Sharks were already leading by ten points.

Province had to hit back hard and fast and they did – thanks to Damian de Allende who burrowed through the Sharks defence, found some space, and strode over the line confidently. The conversion made it ten points to seven. But then a series of penalties to the Sharks saw them stretching their lead out, and at half-time the score was 19 points to 13.

The second half was even more difficult. The Sharks shut down every move that the Province players tried to put together. They won the Currie Cup with a final score of 33 points to 19, and Western Province hung their heads in disappointment.

Despite an incredible first season, after that game all Cheslin could taste was defeat. But he was only 20 years old, and his career had just begun.

# CHAPTER 10

# *A CHAMPIONSHIP YEAR*

Cheslin felt his phone ringing in his pocket. He took it out and smiled when he saw it was his cousin Wayde.

'Wayde! How are you, man?' he answered, 'Long time no hear.'

'Hey Chessie. Where are you? Sounds like somewhere busy.'

'I'm on the Stormers' bus. Coach is taking us on a three-day camp to Hermanus.'

Siya Kolisi nudged Cheslin. 'Is that Wayde? Tell him I say howzit.'

Cheslin nodded as he brought his cousin up to date. He was delighted to be part of the Stormers camp going into the 2014 pre-season. It was another step up the professional ladder and this season he was determined to get onto the field.

The first game of the pre-season was scheduled for 1 February against the Bulls in Polokwane, but the real competition kicked off on 22 February, with a game against the Lions.

Stormers coach, Coetzee had put together an impressive squad. It was an awesome mix of experienced players – Schalk Burger, Duane Vermeulen, Jean de Villiers and Gio Aplon – alongside some fresh and hungry young talent from the under-21 squad, such as himself, Sikhumbuzo Notshe and Oli Kebble.

The standard was high and Cheslin could feel his own game improving all the time.

'That's what happens when you are surrounded by players who are more experienced than you,' he told Wayde.

It was good to catch up on Wayde's news, too. Wayde had been training hard for the 2014 Commonwealth Games in Scotland. He was focusing all his attention on the 400 metres and his training was starting to pay off.

The cousins made a promise to meet up as soon they could, although they knew that it would be some time before either of them could take time out of his schedule.

Hermanus was the perfect place for pre-season fine tuning; not too far from Cape Town, beautiful and quiet with few distractions. The team settled in quickly and got down to work. They had been working hard on their conditioning and now they turned their attention towards the more technical aspects of the game. Cheslin was looking forward to getting his skills razor-sharp.

But life does not always play ball the way you want it to. In the late afternoon of that first day, Cheslin took a low pass, scooping up the ball and darting towards a gap. He sidestepped to the right and narrowly avoided a tackle but misjudged the distance from a teammate and they crashed into each other. Cheslin felt something in his knee give way as he hit the ground.

A wave of pain and dread rose through his body. Not this. Not now. Not when he was so close to starting for the Stormers. But soon the physical agony overwhelmed him. The physiotherapist and his teammates crowded around and then picked him up lightly and carried him off the field.

A visibly upset Coetzee told the media that evening that Cheslin needed a small operation and that he would probably be out of action for two months. To have that kind of accident just days before the season begins is every coach's worst nightmare.

For Cheslin, it was a crushing blow to miss most of the Super Rugby season, but he was determined not to sit around and mope. He found ways to keep busy – playing putt-putt with his leg strapped up, visiting the Waterfront, going on trips to Betty's Bay – and, of course, working out in the gym as much as possible.

Cheslin also discovered that being injured was the perfect time to strike up a romance. He met a beautiful girl called Layla Cupido and the two of them hit it off straight away. Layla was a Capetonian, had attended Pinelands High School and was studying to be a chartered accountant.

By early May Cheslin was fit and ready for

action. He made his on-field debut at Newlands, in a Stormers game against the Highlanders.

He knew his teammates were anxious to see if he still had a spring in his step, and he wanted to put their minds at ease. So, in the opening few minutes of the game, he gathered a high kick and sidestepped two of his opponents, leaving them in the dust. The crowd roared their approval. Cheslin was back and he was better than ever!

However, despite their best efforts, the Stormers could not make any headway that season. They lost six of their first seven games, and although the second half of the season was better, it was too little, too late, and they were forced to watch the knockout rounds on television, like everyone else.

After the Super Rugby campaign came the 2014 Currie Cup. The team shrugged off their disappointment and pulled together, and the result was a triumph for Western Province. They moved like a steamroller through the qualifying rounds, winning eight of the ten games and finishing top of the log. During the tournament, Cheslin scored five tries and one conversion to end up with 27 points for the season.

The home crowds responded well, filling the stands with supporters, singing and cheering after every point they scored. On average, 20 000 fans turned up per game, swelling to over 44 000 people at the final – all looking forward to seeing their heroes lift the trophy.

The final against the Golden Lions was a tense affair. The opposition stuck to their plan to keep it tight and not make any mistakes. Cheslin, playing fullback, knew that he was going to have to prove himself.

In the first half, Western Province played well, putting points on the board. Demetri Catrakilis converted two penalties in the first ten minutes, and then converted a try in the 36th minute. On the other side of the field, flyhalf Maritz Boshoff could not find his form, missing two kickable attempts that left his team losing with a score of 13 points to nil at half-time.

After a tongue-lashing from their coach,

the Lions came into the second half with a new spring in their step. Boshoff got an early penalty over, and then his team put together a long string of passes, ending with Jaco van der Walt going over the line in the corner, despite a desperate tackle from Seabelo Senatla.

The game got increasingly tight. Another penalty given away brought the score to 13–13. The crowd fell silent. Were all the triumphs of the season going to amount to nothing for Western Province?

Jean de Villiers put an arm around Cheslin and urged him to make one final effort. Despite their exhaustion, the Province team pushed play back up into the Lions half. They forced a few errors, and Catrakilis's perfect performance gave them a six-point lead. The Lions fought back hard but it was not enough.

With a final score of 19 points to 16, Western Province were the Currie Cup champions. Cheslin's whole body ached at the end of the game, but when he lifted the trophy over his head in front of the crowd, the pain melted

The 2014 Currie Cup! Winning that was a dream come true.

away. He pictured his proud parents in the stands, and for a moment, it felt like the sun shone brighter just for him.

# CHAPTER 11

## *SEEING THE WORLD*

In many ways, the life of a professional sports-person is not at all glamorous, especially during the season. Typically, they train six days a week with one day off to do publicity for the club or to take care of commitments to sponsors.

They must be disciplined, train hard, watch what they eat and spend hours waiting or travelling between venues, and there is always the threat of injury. It gets lonely at times, and it can be boring too.

Of course, the thrill of running out into a full stadium where everyone knows your name and cheers your every good move makes up for the slog, isolation and pain.

The strongest friendships are usually between athletes who must stick to the same tough schedule. Cheslin became good friends with

Juan de Jongh during his time at Western Province and the club started to feel like a second family to him. He knew that his teammates always had his back – and they knew he would do anything for them.

At times Cheslin's commitment to playing rugby sevens, as well as the 15-man game, made things particularly tough for him. He had to try to work flexibly within the structures of both sports. Luckily, Western Province management understood, and gave him permission to do both.

Being part of the Springbok rugby sevens team provided Cheslin with a wonderful opportunity to see the world. He took it all in, making an effort to understand the people and way of life in whichever city he was visiting – Dubai, Tokyo, Las Vegas or Moscow – and he spent hours on the phone telling Layla about it. Their relationship had gone from strength to strength, and Cheslin thought he had probably met the love of his life.

Although he only scored ten points that

season, Cheslin began to show maturity as a player. He made his presence felt, often gathering the ball deep in his own half before finding a gap, running half the length of the field, and delivering a match-winning pass. He was fierce on defence and creative on attack; and when he had space, his acceleration, sidestep and out-of-the-box thinking made him especially valuable for the Stormers.

His team played well all season and qualified for the quarter-finals of the Super 15. But they came up short against the Brumbies, who beat them by 39 points to 19, with Cheslin scoring the Stormers' only try that day. Cheslin began daring to hope that if he kept this up, a Springbok call-up was a distinct possibility.

But South Africa was blessed with so many good backline players that he could not take it for granted. Guys like Makazole Mapimpi, Lukhanyo Am, Damian de Allende and Sbu Nkosi were all world-class players, hungry to represent their country.

There would be no easy way to the top. Week

in and week out, Cheslin would have to play his best, hoping that he would peak at the right time and remain injury-free. He would do the best he could and leave the rest in God's hands.

# CHAPTER 12

# *SOME DREAMS COME TRUE*

Professional sports can take an athlete from the highest of highs to the lowest of lows in seconds. One moment a player scores a goal and feels on top of the world, and the next, the team loses, and everyone hits rock bottom.

That is why something like the Olympic Games can be a rollercoaster ride. Fourteen days with the whole world watching can be magical and terrifying, all at once.

Rugby had not been part of the Olympics since 1924, but in 2016 rugby sevens would make its debut in Rio de Janeiro. The four top teams from the 2014–15 Sevens World Series qualified. They included South Africa, and Cheslin was over the moon to be going to Rio as part of the team. When he saw that Wayde van Niekerk would also be representing South Africa, he was even more excited.

The cousins shared an emotional hug at the airport as the team gathered and prepared to leave.

'Been too long since we were on a team together, right?' said Wayde.

'Definitely. Way too long.' agreed Cheslin.

'Remember those games in the street when we were kids? Who would have thought we would both be going to the Olympics?'

'Come on, man, be honest,' said Cheslin. 'We both thought it.'

'That's true. We thought we were invincible in those days,' Wayde laughed, looking around to see who else had arrived. 'Come Chessie. Let me introduce you to Caster and Chad.'

★★★

Being in Rio for the Olympics was even better than Cheslin had imagined it would be. The crowds, the city, the passion and the Olympic Village all felt like something out of a movie.

The sevens tournament took place from 6 to 11 August 2016 at the Deodoro Stadium. South

Africa was drawn in a group with France, Spain and Australia. Mainly thanks to their powerful defence, they finished top, only conceding 12 points during the three games.

The quarter-finals were scheduled for four days later. During the break, the team was able to watch some incredible athletes in action. Wayde and Cheslin spent as much time together as possible, connecting like they did when they were kids.

In the quarter-final game, South Africa put on a world-class performance, cruising past Australia with a score of 22 points to five. The only downer was an injury to Seabelo Senatla, which meant that Francois Hougaard would replace him in the semi-final against England the following day.

After their victory against Australia, South Africa looked set to win. But all the flow and co-ordination seemed to desert the Blitzboks. England succeeded in shutting down every attacking move, and a try from Kyle Brown was the only score from either side before half-time.

A few minutes into the second half, England levelled the scores and then converted to take a lead of seven points to five; and that was the way the game ended. It was extremely disappointing but there was no time to wallow in defeat. Later that same day, South Africa played Japan in the third-place playoff, earning the Blitzboks an Olympic bronze medal.

With that over, Cheslin could relax a little and support Wayde. Little did he know that his cousin was about to surprise everyone by exploding dramatically onto the world athletics stage.

During the 400-metre heats Wayde's performance was modest but strong enough to qualify him for the final race. For the final, Wayde was drawn in the outside lane. Cheslin knew it would have been far better for him to start from a position where he could see the other runners.

But Cheslin need not have worried. Wayde exploded from the starting gun and tore his way around the track. To watching South Africans, it seemed like he was carrying all the country's hopes and dreams with him in every step – the kind of motivation that just had to end in a gold medal.

A mere 43.03 seconds later and Wayde had set a new African record, new Olympic record and new world record. Cheslin could scarcely believe it. His cousin had run the fastest 400-metres race of all time. He thought his heart would burst with pride.

★★★

It had become clear to Cheslin that, every time he went away, there was one person he thought about constantly and could not wait to see again – Layla. On the plane home, Cheslin decided. It was time to take their relationship to the next level.

After Cheslin got back from the Olympics he threw himself into Western Province's preparations for the Currie Cup. Disappointingly, they lost the first two games of the season, but they came back strongly with wins against Eastern Province and the Natal Sharks.

On 30 September, Western Province took on the Boland team at Newlands. It was a hard-fought game that Province narrowly won with a score of 30 points to 28.

Normally, the butterflies in Cheslin's stomach disappeared when the game started. That day, the butterflies were worse as the final whistle blew. But it had nothing to do with rugby; this was personal. Cheslin had set something up for the end of the game and he hoped very much it was going to work.

As the crowds emptied out of the stadium, most of the players continued to mill around on the field. They appeared to be waiting for something.

Finally, Layla came onto the field with Rachel, Siya Kolisi's wife. The Province cheerleaders had lined up and started performing and Layla found herself being propelled through their ranks towards Cheslin, who approached nervously and kissed her. As Layla suddenly realised what was happening, her legs buckled for a second and she had to steady herself on Cheslin's arm.

Someone handed Cheslin a tiny box and he went down on one knee in the middle of the field. The crowd that had gathered around them drew closer, clapping and cheering. Layla's family and friends were standing in front, wearing white T-shirts with 'SAY YES' printed on them.

Cheslin opened the box, pulled out a ring and put in on Layla's finger. 'Will you marry me?'

'Yes,' said Layla.

He leapt up, kissed her again and then it all became a blur of confetti, kisses and hugs as everyone congratulated the newly engaged couple.

Cheslin had never been happier and more relieved in his life. The girl of his dreams was now his fiancée, and a wedding date was set.

This life-changing event was soon followed by another.

In April 2016, the Stormers coach, Allister Coetzee had been promoted to Springbok coach with a four-year contract. Coetzee had been part of the Springbok setup many years earlier, but this was the first time he would be coaching the team.

Cheslin had been pleased about the news because it meant that the coach who would be picking the Springbok team would know all about him and his style of playing. He hoped it was a good sign that he would soon graduate to the national team.

Barely three weeks after Cheslin's engagement to Layla, his dream was fulfilled. When Coetzee announced his Springbok squad for the Barbarians tour to England in November, he included 12 outstanding young players as a reward for their excellent form in that year's competitions … and one of them was Cheslin Kolbe.

Cheslin proposes to Layla on the field after a game.

# CHAPTER 13

# *FROM DREAM TO NIGHTMARE*

Cheslin seemed to be following a fairy-tale road to the top.

'The match against the Barbarians is a great opportunity for them to show that they belong at this level,' said Coetzee about his young stars. 'My advice to them is to make it impossible for me to ignore them for future selections.'

At a Springbok training camp in Johannesburg, Cheslin enjoyed getting to know some of the guys he had been playing against for years. He pushed himself in training, learned the coaching staff's plans off by heart and made sure that he was ready to be called on when the opportunity came.

Although the Springbok squad was impressive, 2016 had been a terrible year for them. They had been thumped by the All Blacks, lost to Ireland for the first time on South African soil, and suffered a first-time defeat by Argentina. Cheslin could sense an uncomfortable anxiety and lack of confidence among the players as they gathered at the airport for their flight to London, and their first game in England – against the Barbarians.

The Barbarians game is always a big deal in world rugby. Players are invited from all over the world to play together for just a few weeks. They have a proud and long history and it is a huge honour to be invited.

Cheslin would have loved to play against the Barbarians, but Coetzee selected Jesse Kriel as fullback instead. It was an entertaining game, with the lead going back and forth, ending in a 31–31 draw.

The second game of the tour was against England and Cheslin was once again disappointed not to be selected for the squad. He watched miserably from the stands as England cruised to an easy victory, winning by 37 points to 21. South Africa's team had fallen apart, showing embarrassing weaknesses in many areas of the game.

A week later, the Springboks travelled to Italy and Coetzee selected Willie le Roux as fullback. Once again, Cheslin would play no part in the game.

The team had worked hard all week, but they kept on making silly mistakes, passing the ball into touch, fumbling it when they were attacking and missing tackles. The Italians were full of confidence and the match ended with Italy up by two points. Their crowd went crazy – a victory against the Springboks was something they had only ever dreamed about.

The mood in the Springbok camp had never been worse. Tempers were flaring and everybody seemed to have a different opinion on how to fix their problems.

With one game left – in Cardiff against Wales – rugby lovers in South Africa were fearing the worst. Wales was a strong side. Would there be three defeats in a row?

Although Cheslin tried to keep his spirits up,

and long phone calls to his dad, Layla, and his friends back home helped, he felt strongly affected by his teammates' mood and being overlooked by Coetzee. He was plagued by insecurities. Maybe he simply was too small to play international rugby, and no amount of training or speed would ever change that. Maybe he should just accept that sevens games and provincial games were as high as he would go.

When he saw that Johan Goosen had been chosen as fullback for the final match, he realised he would never have a part in Coetzee's plans. It was a real punch to the gut, and Cheslin wondered why the coach had bothered to bring him on tour. If the Springboks had been a winning team and Coetzee did not want to mess with a winning formula, Cheslin would have understood better.

The game against Wales started off well enough, with Elton Jantjies scoring two penalties, but Wales answered with four penalties of their own, plus two tries in the second half. The Boks made so many errors that they lost with a score of 27 points to 13; their fans' worst fears were realised.

Cheslin's supporters were furious that so many other players had been given a turn at fullback, yet Cheslin had never had a chance to play. Coetzee tried to justify his selection decisions, saying that he had wanted to play everyone on the tour, but it just had not worked out.

It was a tough time for Cheslin. Thinking back to his last season with the Stormers, with Coetzee as coach, he realised that the coach had never allowed him to play his natural game there, either. Every time he got the ball, his instinct was to take on the defenders and gain a few metres, but Coetzee had always instructed him to simply punt the ball back up the field.

Cheslin thought back to his meeting with Olivier Roumat all those years ago. Roumat had told him that he should consider going to play his rugby in France. At the time, Cheslin had worried that it would mean he would not be eligible to play for the Springboks. But Coetzee was contracted to be Springbok coach until 2020, and Cheslin decided he had to be realistic and accept that his Springbok dream was unlikely to come true any time soon.

He had tried to stay positive and committed to the team, but something had to give. He knew he had other options as a professional player, and he could still have a good career. The time was right to make the move.

# CHAPTER 14

## *MOVING TO FRANCE*

Cheslin played his final season for the Stormers during 2017 while his move to France was being finalised. He had been offered a contract by one of the most successful French teams, Toulouse, in the south of the country.

In truth, rugby was not the most important thing on his mind that year. In March, Layla gave birth to an adorable baby girl, Kylah. Cheslin had become a father. When he took his daughter home, he felt amazed that it was possible to love someone so much, so quickly. He already knew that he would do anything for Kylah. He felt certain that moving to Toulouse was right for his family.

Cheslin's last game at Newlands in late July was an emotional experience, but he was too busy to dwell on it. He needed to sort out work visas, sell his car and pack up his whole life in Cape Town. He was also taking French lessons to prepare for working with French-speaking teammates.

In their final game of the season, Stormers lost the quarter-final to Chiefs. After the game, Cheslin stood in the middle of the field, saluting all the fans who had supported him for five years. His mind went back to the moment when he had first run out onto the field for Western Province, and how much had changed since then.

He dreaded saying goodbye to his teammates. Management had organised a trip to Langebaan for the whole team after the season was officially over, and Cheslin went up with Layla. He quietly thanked each person individually for what they had done for him and promised to stay in touch.

At last, everything was packed, all goodbyes were said, and it was time to move forward and embrace their new life in the south of France. Cheslin felt excited. He was only 23 years old and there was still so much to experience.

It was nerve-racking to arrive in a completely strange country after the long journey. Cheslin and Layla were grateful to be greeted by a friendly face in Toulouse. They were just getting settled into their new accommodation when there was a knock on the door. Cheslin opened it to find a big guy with a huge smile.

'Howzit,' he said. 'You must be Cheslin. I'm Maks. Maks van Dyk.'

'It's nice to know there's another South African here,' said Cheslin, looking up at the prop.

'You probably don't remember me, but I was at Paarl Boys' High when you were at Brackenfell.'

'Seriously?'

'Yup. I remember playing a game against you guys. You ran rings around our defence,' said Maks and Cheslin laughed.

'I'm glad we're on the same team, now.'

'Me too,' Cheslin replied. 'What's Toulouse like?'

'You're going to love it here. Come, let me show you guys around.'

The beautiful red brick buildings in Toulouse were glowing a soft pink in the sunset. Cheslin and Kayla admired the churches, town square and canal.

'I think I'm going to like it here,' Layla whispered, squeezing Cheslin's hand.

Cheslin did, too, and he felt even more sure of it the next day when he met the coaching staff and players and saw the club's world-class facilities. He got down to work quickly with the team, as there was not much time before their first game against Oyonnax.

Cheslin wanted to make a good impression in that first game and get the fans on his side. He knew there had been a little gossip in the press, the usual stuff about him being too small for French rugby. The only way to shut them up was to get some points on the board.

But his team struggled that first match in the bright French sunlight. With five minutes to go, Toulouse was trailing, with a score of

23 points to 16. Then the scrumhalf gathered the ball ten metres from the try line and ran sideways, trying to find a gap. He was taken down, but the forwards mauled over the ball and kept it alive, gaining another few metres.

Cheslin hovered on the wing as the ball came towards him – first one pass, then another, and it was in his hands. But there was no space left and the Oyonnax forwards were closing in.

Cheslin held on tight, diving forwards and dotting the ball down over the line just as he was hit hard into the sideline. He bounced up and stuck his hand up in the air, claiming the try. The linesman took a close look and agreed. Cheslin had scored in his first game and earned his team a draw of 23–23.

That first game settled his nerves completely.

'I can feel this is where I'm supposed to be,' he told Layla later that evening, and she agreed.

It was a great season for Cheslin. He scored ten tries for his new team, and they ended up in third place in the league.

Meanwhile, back at home, things had been

changing fast. In February, after a disastrous run, Coetzee had been removed as head coach of the Springbok team. A month later, Rassie Erasmus was appointed as the new head coach, alongside his job of Director of Rugby at SA Rugby.

Cheslin was pleased with the choice. It was a lot of responsibility to put on one man, but Cheslin trusted Erasmus, and knew what a brilliant brain he had for rugby. He thought that the coach might look beyond size and see how well he had been playing in France.

He tried not to get his hopes up, but in his heart, he still believed that he was good enough to play for the Springboks.

# CHAPTER 15

# *THE CALL COMES AT LAST*

It was a magical day in December 2017 when Cheslin and Layla tied the knot on a wine farm outside Stellenbosch, surrounded by friends and family. Layla looked gorgeous. In the speeches, Cheslin was honoured for his humility, respect and discipline.

'They are absolutely amazing together, as a couple,' Layla's mother Renee Cupido said at the wedding.

'I'm really happy to be able to share this beautiful day with them,' said Dillyn Leyds, Stormers fullback, speaking for all Cheslin's teammates.

Cheslin was so happy; he had tears in his eyes more than once during the celebrations. A life goal completed; the only thing that could make things better was a call-up to the Springbok team.

The first test for the Springboks and their new coach was the 2018 Rugby Championship against New Zealand, Australia and Argentina. Erasmus had named Cheslin's good friend Siya Kolisi as the new Springbok captain.

The squad was made up of some dynamic rugby players, such as Sbu Nkosi and Makazole Mapimpi on the wing, and Willie le Roux as fullback – but there was still no place for Cheslin. After such a good season in France, it was hard for him not to show his disappointment.

The Championship kicked off in Durban when the Boks took on Argentina. Since the humiliating defeat in Buenos Aires, they knew not to underestimate this team. Argentina had been improving steadily over the years and were now a serious force in rugby.

But the Boks kept it tight, did the simple things well and earned a victory. Lukhanyo Am, Makazole Mapimpi and Aphiwe Dyantyi all scored tries, and it was wonderful to see the Bok backline playing so well.

Two weeks later, in Argentina, it was a

different story. The Pumas had regrouped, revised their tactics and came at the Springboks ferociously. They forced them into errors, kept them on the back foot and put plenty of points on the board. The Puma flyhalf Nicolás Sánchez was amazing. He scored a try, three conversions, a penalty and a dropkick to give his side a well-earned victory over the Boks of 32 points to 19.

It was a painful defeat for the Springboks. For Cheslin, however, the game provided an unforeseen opportunity. Mapimpi was injured, which left Erasmus short of attacking talent for the rest of the tournament.

Back in Toulouse, Cheslin arrived for a team meeting early one Monday morning after playing a tough weekend game. The forwards coach, William Servat, approached him and sat down.

'How's it going, Cheslin?' he asked.

'Fine, thanks. And with you?' replied Cheslin, slightly puzzled.

'OK, thanks. So, I just want to know something. Can you bring some biltong for me when you come back from South Africa?'

'Um, OK. Sure ...'

He was not planning on a trip home, but Layla was visiting her parents, and he thought that he could ask her to bring some biltong back with her.

Servat got up and wandered off.

'Hey, Coach. Good to see you,' Cheslin greeted Ugo Mola, who had just walked in. The coach just held up his hand to say 'Wait!' and walked towards the rest of the team.

'What's going on?' Cheslin wondered. 'Why is everyone being so weird?'

During the meeting, Mola spoke about the team's performance on the weekend, what they needed to work on during the week, and a little about their opposition.

As everyone filed out after the meeting, Mola asked Cheslin to stay behind. Now Cheslin was sure that he had done something wrong, but what?

Suddenly, he figured it out.

'I'm being dropped for the next game, right?'

Cheslin decided to come straight to the point.

'What are you talking about?' Mola frowned.

'Everyone is acting strangely this morning, and now I know why. I'm being dropped.'

The coach chuckled. 'I can't believe you haven't heard yet. Rassie Erasmus called this morning. He asked if you could join the Springbok team as soon as possible.'

Cheslin's eyes widened. 'Are you joking?'

'Of course not. I told him we'd be sorry to see you go but he's one hundred per cent right. You deserve to be in the Bok team.'

Cheslin gaped at his coach. The chance he had been longing for had finally arrived. He rushed home to pack a few things and caught the next flight to join the Springbok tour in Brisbane, Australia.

★★★

Cheslin immediately threw himself into training. The mood was wonderfully relaxed, so different from the last time he had toured with the national team. When the players were announced, Cheslin saw that he was on the bench. He hoped that he would get a chance to show what he could do. Mapimpi was still in the starting line-up, but with his injury he probably would not be able to play a full game.

The game started badly, with Australia scoring a try in the first minute. But the Boks kept calm and came back strongly. They levelled the score in the 13th minute and took the lead in the 27th minute when Mapimpi went over the line. But in the process, he hurt himself again and the coach turned to Cheslin.

'You ready, Ches? This is it.'

Cheslin stripped off his tracksuit and within minutes was on the pitch and making his Springbok debut. For a second, he thought of his dad at home, watching him, and imagined his joy. Then it was game on, and everything else flew out of his brain.

It was a tight game, but the Wallabies edged ahead by two points, with ten minutes to go. The Boks threw everything they had at them but lost with a score of 23 points to 18. It was not quite the debut Cheslin had hoped for, but still.

A week later Cheslin was back in action against the mighty All Blacks. It was a game that would go down in history. He came on at half-time, with the Boks leading by 24 points to 17. Earlier they had been trailing by 12 points to nil, so it was an incredible fightback.

Two minutes after he came on, Cheslin was defending on the half-way line as the All Blacks swung the ball down towards their winger. Cheslin positioned himself perfectly to intercept a pass with a tap, gather the ball in and set off for the try line. Beauden Barrett started to chase but did not stand a chance of catching him.

Cheslin dotted down, did a little tumble, and punched the air as Willie le Roux gathered him in a giant bear hug. Cheslin's first points for the Boks – what a feeling!

After another try from Aphiwe Dyantyi the Boks had a 12-point lead with just under twenty minutes to go. Surely, they could hold their lead? But the furious All Blacks pack stormed over the line again, taking the score to 36 points to 29. Then they did it again, and with seven minutes to go were within two points of the Boks.

Wave after wave of All Blacks flew towards the try line, but the Boks held on, defending like warriors, and forcing their opponents to make errors. That day, South Africa earned a victory against New Zealand that no rugby fan would forget, which gave the Springboks the confidence that they could beat anyone.

Cheslin had never felt prouder. He knew that now he had earned his place in the team. Erasmus rewarded him by putting him in the starting line-up for the next two matches, where the Boks beat Australia and nearly upset the All Blacks all over again, losing by just two points.

Again, Cheslin scored a beautiful try, and ended up with ten points in the Championship.

His attacking flair and pace finally earned him a place in the Springbok squad.

# CHAPTER 16

# *A SUCCESSFUL YEAR*

Suddenly, Cheslin's life moved into top gear. As soon as the Championship was over, he was back on duty with Toulouse. His team had come a long way and were having a fantastic season.

In November 2018, he was selected to be part of the Springboks' northern hemisphere tour. They were scheduled to play four matches in three weeks against England, France, Scotland and Wales. The Boks narrowly squeezed past the French in stoppage time to win the first game of that series, then they won a hard-fought match against Scotland the following week. In the final game they came up short against a slick and impressive Wales, who beat them 20 points to 11.

Nevertheless, it was a great tour, and made up

for Cheslin's bad memories from his last European tour. It showed that Erasmus understood his players and the team and was building a strong foundation for the World Cup.

Back in Toulouse, Cheslin's teammates continued to play excellent rugby, with consistent wins. After 26 gruelling rounds of the Top 14 competition, they were ranked the top team in France.

In early June 2019, Cheslin's try in the 65th minute of the semi-final helped Toulouse secure an easy victory of 20 points to six against La Rochelle. Clermont beat Lyon in the other semi-final, and so the final saw a face-off between the two French rugby giants. Cheslin played fullback and another South African, Rynhardt Elstadt, who had recently joined the team, played flanker.

Toulouse were dominant, earning a final score of 24 points to 18. Cheslin was superb on attack and defence, and the local fans made it clear that they embraced him as one of their own.

Lifting the trophy with Toulouse meant as

much to Cheslin as it had done to win the Currie Cup with Western Province. He had made this city his home; he loved it and was loved and supported right back.

Back home in South Africa, everyone was talking about the World Cup, which was just a few months away. The team had improved so much under Erasmus that some said they might even win. The first match they were playing would be the All Blacks, which was a tough draw. But to be the best, you must beat the best.

Before the World Cup there was one more tournament to play. In a short, three-week championship, South Africa would play single games against Argentina, Australia and New Zealand – three games in total. It was a great opportunity for the teams to test their strength and see what areas they still needed to work on.

Erasmus was still trying out various combinations, so Cheslin sat out the game against Australia, which the Boks won.

The following game, against the All Blacks, saw Cheslin on the right wing. The Springboks took an early lead thanks to Handré Pollard's boot, but a simple error moments later let the All Blacks back in for a try and at half-time the Boks trailed six points to seven.

In the second half, New Zealand kept getting penalties and putting them over, and with ten minutes to go they were leading 16 points to nine. Things were not looking good for South Africa.

Then in the final minute, the Boks whipped the ball down the wing to Cheslin, who was around the halfway line. He sped past a few defenders and chipped the ball high towards the try line and Herschel Jantjies. Jantjies jumped up with a defender and the ball bounced off his shoulder and forward; he grabbed it just in time and fell over the line to score a brilliant try.

The pressure was now on Pollard to convert the try and level the scores, which is exactly what he did. What a brilliant game!

In the match against Argentina, Cheslin scored another fine try for the Boks, using his pace to beat the defenders and touch down. The

Boks beat Argentina, and with two wins and one draw they won the championship against the best teams in the southern hemisphere. What better preparation could there possibly be for the World Cup?

And without a doubt, Cheslin's performance would secure him a position on the team.

# CHAPTER 17

# *WORLD CHAMPIONS*

The Springboks wanted to spend as much time as possible getting used to the playing conditions in Japan. So, three weeks before their first game, they were at the airport on their way to Kagoshima, where they would be based.

'Ready for the big time, Ches?' asked Eben Etzebeth.

'Born ready,' he replied.

'Don't give Cheslin a seat with extra leg room,' joked Bongi Mbonambi. 'He doesn't need it.'

'*Ja*, well, you probably need two seats, so I'm not sitting next to you!' Cheslin joked back.

The hard work began immediately on arrival. Thousands of Japanese turned up to watch the Springboks train and stunned the players by knowing the South African national anthem and all about South African culture. Cheslin was impressed by the country and how well organised everything was.

A warm-up match against Japan went well for the Boks and they felt confident that they had done everything they possibly could to prepare. Now it was time to deliver.

However, the first game of the tournament against New Zealand did not go according to plan. This time the All Blacks played a better game and won with a score of 23 points to 13, and there was no shortage of pundits ready to point out that no team had ever won the World Cup after losing the first game.

The Boks paid no attention, and, bouncing right back, they scored 57 points against Namibia's three and then 49 points against Italy's three. Playing against Italy, Cheslin scored twice and was named Man of the Match.

But ten minutes before the end, he twisted his left ankle and had to leave the field. A shiver of dread ran through him as he waited for the physiotherapist. Surely this was not how it was going to end for him?

'The good news is, this won't take long to heal, Ches,' said the physiotherapist and Cheslin breathed a sigh of relief. 'The bad news is, I'm going to hold you back for the next couple of games, just to make sure.'

Cheslin nodded. He knew the team would cruise past Canada – but they would face Japan in the quarter-finals, and the hosts had been playing excellent rugby. But what could he do?

It turned out there was no need to worry. The Springboks stuck to their plan, denying Japan any scoring opportunities, and sending Mapimpi over the line twice to score a victory of 26 points to three.

Cheslin was delighted to be called back into action for the semi-final against Wales. The night before the match, the team gathered to watch England demolish the All Blacks. It was one of the best rugby performances that anyone had ever seen, and the All Blacks had no answer for it.

But the Boks could not spend too much time thinking about that – they had to keep their focus on Wales. Although Wales were tired and had suffered a few key injuries along the way, it was a tight, tense match. As always, Pollard was great with his boot, scoring four out of four penalties, and the Springboks won by three points.

South Africa was headed for the final match against England.

The week leading up to the game felt like a dream. The players tried to stick to their usual routines, but it was hard to not be distracted and to stay calm. They wanted this win so badly, for themselves and for everyone back home.

Most newspapers were stating how good England was to have demolished the All Blacks, and how South Africa, which had lost a pool game, was unlikely to win the World Cup. The Springboks knew they were the underdogs.

Now, suddenly, here they were, on the field, in front of the glaring lights and the restless crowd. For the next 80 minutes, the whole team had to play as if their lives depended on it. And play they did.

The Boks were in the lead the entire game. The forward pack sent the English backwards repeatedly, winning penalty after penalty. Each kick was handled by Pollard in his calm and collected manner.

The rock-solid Springbok defence frustrated every English attack. First, Makazole Mapimpi and Lukhanyo Am teamed up for a beautiful try, giving the team the sense that this was definitely going to be their night. Then, Cheslin used all his old tricks to sidestep the England captain and score, leaving Owen Farrell sprawled out on the grass. That moment sealed the win that would live on in memory.

Cheslin's phone did not stop ringing for days. Everyone wanted to express their love, support and congratulations.

One of the first calls was from Wayde. Cheslin had been there for his cousin when he won Olympic gold and now Wayde wanted to do the same for him.

'Wait until you get back home, Ches,' said

Wayde. 'You won't believe how the people support you and Siya and the whole team. It's incredible.'

And the good news just kept on rolling in.

Cheslin was nominated as World Rugby Player of the Year, alongside players from England, New Zealand, the United States and Wales. Although he lost to teammate Pieter-Steph du Toit, it hardly felt like losing at all.

And a few weeks after that, he received the Player of the Year award at the French Rugby 'Oscars'. As he walked up to accept his award, Cheslin thought about how often he had been told he was too small for this game. He wanted to send a message out to all young boys with the same fear.

'Since the beginning of my professional career, I have heard so many times that I was too small, too light, that I could not go further,' he said in his speech. 'I had the opportunity to prove that these people were wrong. Weight and size are nothing next to what you can accomplish with your determination.'

Still well short of his thirties, Cheslin has so much that he can accomplish, on and off the rugby field. Who knows … he could even be there to lift the next World Cup trophy for the Boks in 2023.

# SOURCES

https://en.wikipedia.org/wiki/Cheslin_Kolbe

https://wprugby.com/

https://www.iol.co.za/sport/opinion/south-african-rugby-
failed-cheslin-kolbe-7453435

https://www.iol.co.za/weekend-argus/watch-cheslin-has-
proved-them-wrong-says-proud-dad-16952315

https://www.rugbyworldcup.com/2019

https://www.sarugbymag.co.za/kolbe-moment-bok-
dream-came-true/

https://www.sport24.co.za/Rugby/SuperRugby/
emotional-farewell-for-cheslin-kolbe-20170802

https://www.telegraph.co.uk/rugby-world-
cup/2019/10/16/cheslin-kolbe-bucked-south-africas-
fetish-bulk-height-prove/

https://www.ultimaterugby.com/toulouse/squad

# *CLASSROOM ACTIVITIES*

## *ORAL ACTIVITIES*

1. Work in pairs. One should play the part of Cheslin Kolbe and one the part of Wayde van Niekerk. Role play a conversation between the cousins about their childhood and their lives now. Talk about their memories and hopes for the future.

2. Work on your own. Imagine you are a friend of Cheslin Kolbe's. You have been asked to give a two-minute speech at Cheslin's wedding. Write the speech and present it to your class.

3. Work on your own. Find out as much as you can about Cheslin Kolbe's famous sidestep and tell your class about it. Use information from this book as well as from your own research.

4.  Work on your own. Choose three matches that you think have been highlights of Cheslin Kolbe's career thus far and tell the class why.

5.  Work in a group. Discuss whether you would like to be a professional sports player. Explain why or why not.

6.  As a class, role play the scene in which Cheslin Kolbe proposes to Layla Cupido. Make sure that each person has a role to play:
    *   Cheslin
    *   Layla
    *   other Western Province team members
    *   Rachel Kolisi
    *   Layla's friends and family.

7.  Work in pairs. Imagine you are a fan of Cheslin Kolbe, and you meet him face to face.
    *   Tell him three things you most admire about him.

- Ask him three things you would like to know about him or his career.
- Take turns to be Cheslin and his fan.